Franz

LISZT

Tasso: Lamento e Trinofo

Symphonic Poem No. 2

S. 96

Study Score

Partitur

PETRUCCI LIBRARY PRESS

INTRODUCTION

The present score is a reissue of one from the Franz Liszt-Stiftung edition, originally published by Breitkopf & Härtel from 1907-1936. The edition was prepared in an effort to publish the entire oeuvre of Franz Liszt. Editors included such prominent musicians as Béla Bartok, Ferruccio Busoni, Eugène d'Albert and José Vianna da Motta – some of whom studied with Liszt – as well as scholars like Peter Raabe, who would later compile the first catalog of the composer's works. The need for a complete edition was already apparent by the time of Liszt's death. Although some of his piano music had regularly appeared in new editions throughout his life, these works were by no means representative of even his pianistic output. A far more unfortunate fate was left for his orchestral music - which would usually be issued only once, soon to go out of print and later scarcely available. The Liszt-Stiftung edition revived many works that had fallen into relative obscurity and was therefore handsomely welcomed.

The edition was sadly never completed. The publication activity was brought to a premature end by the time of the Second World War. All in all the incomplete edition encompassed 34 volumes, among others two symphonies, the symphonic poems, some concert works, a couple of piano arrangements and 11 volumes of original works for piano – a mere fraction of the composer's output – but the edition would nonetheless break the ground for Liszt research during the 20th century for a number of reasons. First, it brought to light a number of late pieces that would put Liszt as a forerunner of experimental music and firmly establish his position as such. Second, it revealed the diversity of Liszt's output, which up until that time had been best known as an important addition to the piano repertoire. Third, it displayed the complex and characteristic nature of many of his works by being the first edition to show and make use of several alternative (sometimes vastly different) versions and sources. Last but not least, it would provide the world with a generally reliable edition of easy availability and very high standard for its day.

The Bavarian State Library acquired a complete copy of said edition and decided to digitize it in 2008. By that time more than 70 years had passed since its publication, effectively rendering the edition out of copyright and free for any use. Each and every page was scanned and uploaded to their online digital collection. While this was a great effort in itself, the site has a rudimentary interface, is difficult to navigate and the scores are not in the context of relevant information. One of our users decided to also upload it to our site, the International Music Score Library Project (IMSLP) / Petrucci Music Library, the unique wiki-based repository of musical scores, composers and indexes that anyone can edit and amend. Through the effort of a single user, Mattias K. (piupianissimo), the entire edition is now easily available worldwide to those who wish to perform and study the composer's music in a historical context, since as the case is with Liszt's music, many early editions exist and many are readily available on the site and many more will be available in the future. IMSLP is as such a valuable resource available to the scholar but even more to the performer who is always a mere mouse click away from scores that have not been in print since the turn of the past century, or that are otherwise hard to come by. The availability, quantity of ease of access for online scores will soon exceed those of the traditional medium of print. Nevertheless new works have always been published through the printed medium and this tradition is going to persist for many years to come even if complemented by the digital medium. Of course an important fact to stress is that the availability of digital scores online does not exclude the need of printed score since neither one can replace the comfort and neatness of one another. The quality of a bound reprint or new engraving exceeds that of a score printed at home.

I discovered IMSLP back in early 2006 when it first began. At that time many scores were scattered on the net either privately or on commercial collection sites. Many of these sites had a considerably large collection but sadly many had restrictions on number of downloads per day and the process of contributing to them was riddled with bureaucracy. IMSLP was the first free site where anyone could contribute and upload any kind of musical scores. I have personally searched and uploaded many works – particularly those of Liszt – and the future of the site is nothing but bright. At the time of its start only a handful of scores were available on the site but through the effort of its users IMSLP has grown to be the largest collection of scores available on the Internet.

Tasso: Lamento e Trionfo is the second work in a series of thirteen symphonic poems composed by Franz Liszt. It was composed from 1849-54 and first published in 1856 by Breitkopf und Härtel of Leipzig. The dedicatee is Princess Carolyne zu Sayn-Wittgenstein. This score is from the first volume of the Franz Liszt-Stiftung edition, edited by Otto Taubmann and was published in 1908. The score, along with a number or arrangements, is also available directly at the following URL:
http://imslp.org/wiki/Tasso:_Lamento_e_Trionfo,_S.96_(Liszt,_Franz)

Soren Afshar (Funper)

Summer, 2011

TASSO
LAMENTO E TRIONFO.
SYMPHONISCHE DICHTUNG No. 2 VON F. LISZT.

Im Jahre 1849 wurde in ganz Deutschland der hundertjährige Geburtstag Goethes durch Feste verherrlicht; das Theater in Weimar, wo wir uns damals befanden, feierte den 28. August durch eine Darstellung des Tasso.

Das herbe Geschick dieses unglücklichen Dichters hat den beiden grössten Poeten, welche Deutschland und England im letzten Jahrhundert hervorbrachten, Stoff zu dichterischen Gebilden gegeben: Goethe und Byron. Goethe, dem das glänzendste Lebensloos fiel, Byron, welchem die Vorzüge des Ranges und der Geburt durch die tiefsten Dichterleiden verkümmert wurden. Wir wollen nicht in Abrede stellen, dass, als wir im Jahre 1849 den Auftrag bekamen, eine Ouvertüre zu Goethes Drama zu schreiben, das ehrfurchtsvolle Mitleid, mit welchem Byron die Manen des grossen Dichters beschwört, einen vorherrschend bestimmenden Einfluss auf unsere Gestaltung dieses Gegenstandes übte. Aber Byron konnte, indem er Tasso im Kerker selbstredend einführt, mit der Erinnerung der tödtlichen Schmerzen, denen er in seiner Klage eine so hinreissende Gewalt edlen Ausdrucks verleiht, nicht das Andenken des Triumphes verbinden, durch welchen dem ritterlichen Sänger des „Befreiten Jerusalem" eine späte aber glänzende Vergeltung ward. Wir wollten diesen Gegensatz schon im Titel des Werkes klar aussprechen und unser Bestreben ging dahin, in Tönen die grosse Antithese des im Leben verkannten, im Tode aber von strahlender Glorie umgebenen Genius zu schildern, von einer Glorie, welche mit vernichtenden Strahlen in die Herzen der Verfolger trifft. Tasso liebte und litt in Ferrara, er wurde in Rom gerächt, und er lebt noch heute in den Volksgesängen Venedigs. Diese drei Momente sind von seinem unvergänglichen Ruhme untrennbar. Um sie musikalisch wiederzugeben, riefen wir zuerst seinen grossen Schatten herauf, wie er noch heute an Venedigs Lagunen wandelt; dann erschien uns sein Antlitz stolz und schwermütig den Festen Ferraras zuschauend, wo er seine Meisterwerke geschaffen, und folgten wir ihm endlich nach Rom, der ewigen Stadt, die ihm die Ruhmeskrone reichte und so den Märtyrer und Dichter in ihm feierte.

TASSO
LAMENTO E TRIONFO.
POÈME SYMPHONIQUE No. 2 DE F. LISZT.

En 1849 l'Allemagne entière célébra avec éclat le centième anniversaire de la naissance de Goethe. A Weimar où nous nous trouvions alors, le programme des fêtes avait marqué la représentation de son drame Le Tasse pour le soir du 28 Août.

Les malheurs de la destinée du plus infortuné des poètes avaient frappé et occupé l'imagination des plus puissants génies poétiques de notre temps, Goethe et Byron; Goethe dont le sort fut entouré des plus brillantes prospérités, Byron dont les avantages de naissance et de fortune furent contrebalancés par de si vives souffrances. Nous ne saurions dissimuler que lorsqu'on nous chargea, en 1849, d'écrire une ouverture pour le drame de Goethe, nous nous sommes plus directement inspirés de la respectueuse compatissance de Byron pour les mânes du grand homme qu'il évoquait, que de l'œuvre du poète allemand. Toutefois, Byron, en nous transmettant en quelque sorte les gémissements du Tasse dans sa prison, n'a pu joindre au souvenir de ses poignantes douleurs si noblement et si éloquemment exprimées en sa Lamentation, celui du Triomphe qui attendait, par une tardive mais éclatante justice, le chevaleresque auteur de la «Jérusalem délivrée». Nous avons voulu indiquer ce contraste dans le titre même de notre œuvre, et eussions souhaité réussir à formuler cette grande antithèse du génie mal traité durant sa vie, et rayonnant après sa mort d'une lumière écrasante pour ses persécuteurs. Le Tasse a aimé et souffert à Ferrare; il a été vengé à Rome; sa gloire est encore vivante dans les chants populaires de Venise. Ces trois moments sont inséparables de son immortel souvenir. Pour les rendre en musique, nous avons d'abord fait surgir la grande ombre du héros telle qu'elle nous apparaît aujourd'hui hantant les lagunes de Venise; nous avons entrevu ensuite sa figure hautaine et attristée glisser à travers les fêtes de Ferrare où il avait donné le jour à ses chefs-d'œuvre; enfin nous l'avons suivi à Rome, la ville éternelle qui, en lui tendant sa couronne, glorifia en lui le martyr et le poète.

TASSO
LAMENTO E TRIONFO.
SYMPHONIC POEM No. 2 BY F. LISZT.

In 1849 the hundredth anniversary of Goethe's birth was celebrated throughout Germany with great splendour. At Weimar, where I then resided, the occasion was marked, on the 28th of August, by a performance of Goethe's Tasso.

The unhappy destiny of the most unfortunate of poets had struck and occupied the imagination of the most powerful poetic geniuses of our time, Goethe and Byron — Goethe, whose lot it was to be surrounded with brilliant prosperity; Byron, whose advantages of birth and fortune were counterbalanced by much suffering. I shall not attempt to deny that I was more immediately inspired by the respectful compassion evoked by Byron for the manes of the great man, than by the work of the German poet. Nevertheless, while making us feel and hear the groans of Tasso in his prison, Byron has not been able to join to the remembrance of the bitter sorrows, so nobly and eloquently expressed in his Lamentation that of the Triumph, which a tardy but brilliant justice was reserving for the chivalrous author of 'Jerusalem Delivered.' I have wished to indicate this contrast even in the title of my work, and have hoped to succeed in portraying this grand antithesis of genius ill-treated during life, and shining after death with a light which should overwhelm its persecutors. Tasso loved and suffered at Ferrara; he was revenged at Rome; his glory still lives in the popular songs of Venice. These three periods are inseparable from his immortal memory. To render these in music, I felt I must first call up the spirit of the hero as it now appears to us, haunting the lagunes of Venice; next, we must see his proud and sad figure, as it glides among the fêtes of Ferrara — the birthplace of his masterpieces; finally, we must follow him to Rome, the Eternal City, which, in holding forth to him his crown, glorified him as a martyr and poet.

Lamento e Trionfo: So heissen die beiden grossen Kontraste im Geschick der Poeten, von denen mit Recht gesagt wurde, dass, ob auch oft mit Fluch ihr Leben belastet werde, nimmer der Segen ausbleibe auf ihrem Grabe. Um aber unsrer Idee nicht allein die strengste Autorität, sondern auch den Glanz der Tatsachen zu verleihen, entlehnten wir selbst die Form zu ihrer künstlerischen Gestaltung aus der Wirklichkeit, und wählten deshalb zum Thema unsres musikalischen Gedichtes die Melodie, auf welche wir venetianische Lagunenschiffer drei Jahrhunderte nach des Dichters Tode die Anfangsstrophen seines **Jerusalems** singen hörten:

Canto l'armi pietose e'l Capitano,
Che'l gran Sepolcro liberò di Cristo!

Das Motiv selbst hat eine langsame Bewegung, es teilt die Empfindung seufzender Klage, monotoner Schwermut mit; die Gondoliere geben ihm aber durch das Ziehen gewisser Töne eine ganz eigentümliche Färbung und die melancholisch gedehnten Klänge machen aus der Ferne einen Eindruck, als wenn lange Streifen verklärten Lichtes vom Wellenspiegel zurückgestrahlt würden. Dieser Gesang hatte uns einst lebhaft ergriffen, und als wir später Tasso musikalisch darstellen sollten, drängte er sich uns gebieterisch zum Text unserer Gedanken auf, als ein immer fortlebender Beweis der Huldigung seiner Nation für den Genius, dessen Treue und Anhänglichkeit Ferrara so schlecht vergalt. Die venetianische Melodie ist so voll von unheilbarer Trauer, von nagendem Schmerz, dass ihre einfache Wiedergabe genügt, um Tassos Seele zu schildern. Sie gibt sich dann, ganz wie die Einbildung des Dichters, den glänzenden Täuschungen der Welt, der trügerischen, gleissenden Koketterie jenes Lächelns hin, dessen Gift die schreckliche Katastrophe herbeiführte, für welche scheinbar keine irdische Vergütung möglich war, und welche dann doch zuletzt auf dem Capitol mit einem Mantel überdeckt wurde, der in einem reineren Purpur glänzte, als der des Alphons. (Übersetzung v. P. Cornelius.)

Lamento e Trionfo: telles sont les deux grandes oppositions de la destinée des poètes, dont il a été justement dit, que si on fait peser parfois la malédiction sur leur vie, la bénédiction ne manque jamais à leur tombe. Afin de donner à cette idée non seulement l'autorité mais l'éclat du Fait, nous avons voulu emprunter au fait sa forme même, et pour cela nous avons pris comme thème de notre poème musical, le motif sur lequel nous avons entendu les gondoliers de Venise chanter sur les lagunes les strophes du Tasse, et redire encore trois siècles après lui:

Canto l'armi pietose e'l Capitano,
Che'l gran Sepolcro liberò di Christo!

Ce motif est en lui-même plaintif, d'une gémissante lenteur, d'un deuil monotone; mais les gondoliers lui prêtent un miroitement tout particulier en traînant certaines notes par la retenue des voix, qui à distance planent et brillent comme des traînées de gloire et de lumière. Ce chant nous avait profondément impressionnés jadis, et lorsque nous eûmes à parler du Tasse, il eût été impossible à notre sentiment ému de ne point prendre pour texte de nos pensées, cet hommage persistant rendu par sa nation à l'homme de génie dont la cour de Ferrare ne méritait ni l'attachement ni la fidélité. Le motif vénitien respire une mélancolie si navrée, une tristesse si irrémédiable, qu'il suffit de le poser pour révéler le secret des douloureuses émotions du Tasse. Il s'est prêté ensuite, tout comme l'imagination du poète, à la peinture des brillantes illusions du monde, des décevantes et fallacieuses coquetteries de ces sourires dont le perfide poison amena l'horrible catastrophe qui semblait ne pouvoir trouver de compensation en ce monde, et qui, néanmoins, fut revêtue au Capitole d'une pourpre plus pure que celle du manteau d'Alphonse!

Lamento e Trionfo: these are the two great contrasts in the destiny of poets, of whom it has been truly said that if fate curses them during life, blessing never fails them after death. In order to give to this idea not only the authority but the splendour of reality, I have endeavoured to borrow even its form from fact; and for this purpose have taken, as the theme of this musical poem, the melody to which, three hundred years after the poet's death, we have heard the gondoliers of Venice sing upon her waters the opening lines of his **Jerusalem**: —

"'Canto l'armi pietose e'l Capitano,
Che'l gran Sepolcro liberò di Cristo!'"

This melody is in itself plaintive, slow, and mournfully monotonous; but the gondoliers give it quite a special character by dragging certain notes and holding out their voices, which, heard from a distance, produce an effect similar to that of rays of light reflected from the ripple of the waves. This song had already so powerfully impressed me, that when the subject of Tasso was suggested to me for musical illustration, I could not but take for the text of my thoughts this enduring homage rendered by his nation to a genius of whom the court of Ferrara had proved itself unworthy. The Venetian melody breathes so gnawing a melancholy, so irremediable a sadness, that a mere reproduction of it seems sufficient to reveal the secret of Tasso's sad emotions. As the imagination of the poet lends itself to depict the brilliant illusions of the world, so this melody seems to express the deceptive and fallacious coquetries of those smiles, whose perfidious poison brought about the horrible catastrophe which could never find compensation in this world, but was, nevertheless, covered at the Capitol with a mantle far exceeding in splendour the purple of Alphonso.

INSTRUMENTATION

2 Flutes
Piccolo
2 Oboes
2 Clarinets (B-flat)
Bass Clarinet (B-flat)
2 Bassoons

4 Horns (B-flat, C)
4 Trumpets (C)
3 Trombones
Tuba

Timpani
Percussion
(Triangle, Snare Drum, Bass Dum, Cymbals)
Harp

Violins I
Violins II
Violas
Violoncellos
Basses

Duration: ca. 21 minutes

First Performance: April 19, 1854
Weimar: Hofkapelle Weimar
Franz Liszt, conductor

ISBN: 978-1-60874-022-2

This score is an unabridged reprint of the score
first issued in Leipzig by Breitkopf & Härtel, 1908. Plate F. L. 3

Printed in the USA
First Printing: August, 2011

TASSO: LAMENTO E TRIONFO

Symphonic Poem No. 2

S. 96

FRANZ LISZT (1811–1886)

Der Buchstabe R.... bedeutet ein geringes Ritardando, so zu sagen: ein leises crescendo des Rhythmus.
The letter R.... signifies a slight Ritardando, that is to say: a soft crescendo of the rhythm.
La lettre R.... signifie un petit Ritardando, c'est-à-dire: un doux crescendo du rhythme.

R
molto dim.
espressivo
a 2.
dim.
molto dim.
molto dim.
molto dim.
molto dim.
pizz.
molto dim.
R

mf
Solo
rinf.
rinf.
mf
dim.
dim.
dim.
dim.
dim.
dim.
dim.
dim.
dim.
dim.
dim.
dim.
rinf
rinf
rinf
rinf
pizz.
pizz.
pizz.
f
f
f

A Allegro strepitoso.
accelerando
cresc.
p
cresc.
f
mf
mf pesante
arco
A Allegro strepitoso.

Muta in E.

marcato agitato
marcato agitato
marcato agitato
div.

rinf.
tr
cresc.
rinf.
cresc. e sempre più agitato e stringendo

sempre più rinf. ed agitato
sempre più rinf. ed agitato
sempre più rinf. ed agitato
sempre più rinf. ed agitato
tr
Muta in Es. As.
ff
ff
ff
ff

Lento.
ritard.
Lunga Pausa.
sf
sf
sf
sf
Solo
f
Solo
mf
dim. e rit. pp
f
f espress.
Lento.
ritard.
Lunga Pausa.

Ein C.-Bass, die übrigen tacent. *Only one C.-Bass, the remaining tacent.* Une C.-basse seulement, les autres tacent.

*) In Ermangelung der Bassklarinette ist das Motiv durch 3 Violoncelle auszuführen.
Where a bass-clarinet is not available the motive is to be executed by three violoncellos.
Faute de basse-tube, le motif sera exécuté par trois violoncelles.

(f)
rit.
pp
pp
Muta in C.
pp
f
6
f
rit.
(p)
(f)
rit.
a 3.
(p)
rit.
(p)
rit.

smorz.
pp
smorz.
Muta in E.
pp
p
p
p
p
f
f
3
3
3
divisi
espressivo
p
arco
p
arco
p

rit.

pp
smorz.
pp
smorz.
pp
smorz.
pp
smorz.
dim.
pp
pp
pp
I.
Vcelle.
II.u.III.
pp
pp
Solo.
(p)
espress. molto

p
dolce
Solo.
in C.
dolce espress. molto
in Es. As.
pp
6
p
divisi
arco

C
R
p
p
pp
pp
Muta in E H.
divisi
p espr.
6
cresc.
cresc.
6
C
R

p
p
p
p
pizz.
p
Tutti.
pizz.
p
pizz.
p
arco

unis.
divisi a 3.
arco

un poco accelerando
cresc. e più agitato
cresc. e più agitato
un poco accelerando

cresc.
cresc.
rinf.
a 2.

poco rit.

dim. molto

pp

Solo.

espressivo

in C.

dim.

in E.

dim.

poco rit.

D Meno Adagio.
in E.
f con grandezza
f
f
ff
pizz.
f
pizz.
f
f
f
pizz.
f
D Meno Adagio.

f
f
arco
rinf.
arco
rinf.
rinf.
rinf.
arco
rinf.
pizz.
pizz.
pizz.

a 2.
marc.
marc.
marc.
in E.H.
arco
arco
arco

Solo.
p
marc.
marc.
marc.
ff
Muta in C.
Muta in Es. B.

E
Recitativo, espressivo assai
Solo.
p espressivo
divisi
trem.
p
trem.
p
E

p
cresc.
a 2.
a 2.
f
cresc
cresc.
in Es. B.
div.

a 2.
Muta in A.
a 2.
Muta in D.
Muta in Es.
in C.
a 2.
a 2.
Muta in C. G.

Allegretto mosso con grazia (quasi Menuetto).
pizz.
pizz.
2 Vcelle Soli.
mf espressivo
Die übr. Vcelle.
pizz.
pizz.
Allegretto mosso con grazia (quasi Menuetto).

p

p

F sempre tranquillo
a 2.
sempre piano
sempre piano
Solo.
p espressivo
sempre piano
in Es.
p
dolce
pizz.
p
pizz.
p
arco
pizz.
p
pizz.
p
F sempre tranquillo

a 2.
p
Solo.
p
sempre p
in D.
p
dolce
pizz.
arco
pizz.

pizz.
arco

pizz.
arco

espressivo
Solo.
a 2.
espressivo
Solo.
espress.
arco
pizz.
espressivo
arco
pizz.
arco
pizz.
arco
arco
tr

a 2.
a 2.
tr
tr
tr

Hier nimmt der Vortrag des Orchesters einen doppelten Charakter an: die Bläser leicht und flatterhaft; die singenden Streich-Instrumente sentimental und graziös.

Here the orchestra assumes a dual character: the wind-instruments lightly and flutteringly; the cantabile stringed instruments sentimentally and gracefully.

L'exécution de l'orchestre prendici un double caractère: lesjoueurs d'instruments à vent d'une façon légère et volage, les instruments chantants à archet d'une façon sentimentale et gracieuse.

a 2.
arco
arco
pizz.
pizz.
marcato
marcato

a 2.
espressivo cantando
p
a 2.
espressivo cantando
espressivo
arco
pizz.
marcato
marcato

a 2.
marcato
marcato

a 2.
Solo.
arco
arco
arco
p
p

poco rit.
G Poco a poco più di moto.
a 2.
cantando espressivo
dim.
a 2.
cantando espressivo
dim.
p
Muta in B basso
dim.
in Es.
p
in C.
p il canto espressivo
p dolce
p dolce
poco rit.
dim.
p
p
p
mf
arco
mf
poco rit.
G Poco a poco più di moto.

a 2.
tr
tr

a 2.
in B basso
a 2.
p
f
tr

f
tr
tr

accelerando
cresc. molto
cresc. molto
cresc. molto
cresc. molto
a 2.
f marcato
Muta in C.
accelerando
a 2.
f marcato
cresc.
cresc.
in C. G.
p
cresc.
molto cresc.
divisi
accelerando
cresc. molto rinf.
div.
cresc. molto rinf.
div.
cresc. molto rinf.
cresc. molto rinf.
cresc. molto rinf.
accelerando

Allegro strepitoso.

Allegro strepitoso.

a 2.
p
p
fp
fp
tr
fp
marcato agitato
f
marcato agitato
mf
f
marcato agitato
p
ff
ff

*) Die Klarinetten sind in den Orchesterstimmen bis zum Buchstaben H (Allegro con molto brio) in A zu transponieren.
The clarinets in the orchestral parts up to the letter H (Allegro con molto brio) to be transposed into A.
Dans les parties d'orchestre, les clarinettes sont à transposer en La jusqu'à la lettre H (Allegro con molto brio).

sempre più rinf. ed agitato

sempre più rinf. ed agitato

sempre più rinf. ed agitato

sempre più rinf. ed agitato

tr

ff

ff

ff

ff

Muta in G.

rit.
Lento assai.
sf
sf
sf
a 2.
Muta in C.
ff
dim.
smorz.
ff
dim.
smorz.
rit.
ff
dim. smorz.
ff
dim. smorz.
rit.
Lento assai.

H Allegro con molto brio.
in C.
a 2.
mf
in G.
cresc.
f
H
Allegro con molto brio.

stacc.
stacc.
stacc.
stacc.
stacc.
p
p
p
p
pizz.
p

arco
pizz.
arco

pizz.
arco
pizz.
arco

mf
p
p
p
pizz.

I
a 2.
f
a 2.
f
a 2.
f
a 2.
f
stacc.
a 2.
(mf)
(mf)
a 2.
(mf)
(mf)
arco
cresc.
cresc.
I

rf
rf
cresc.
rf
rf
rf
rf

div.
pizz.
pizz.

dim.

(p)

dim.

(p)

dim.

p legero

arco

p legero

dim.

p legero

a 2.

a 2.

a 2.

arco

J
ff
a 2.
tr
J ff

tr
ff

K
Poco a poco più mosso sin al quasi Presto.
p
mf
p
p
mf
a 2.
mf nobile
mf
p
p
p
pizz.
p
pizz.
p
K
Poco a poco più mosso sin al quasi Presto.

a 2.

pp
cresc.
p
mf
tr
div.
arco

L
f e più cresc.
f e più cresc.
f e più cresc.
f e più cresc.
f e più cresc.
a 2.
f e più cresc.
a 2.
f e più cresc.
f e più cresc.
f e più cresc.
f e più cresc.
f e più cresc.
f e più cresc.
tr
f
cresc
f e più cresc.
f e più cresc.
f e più cresc.
L

Quasi Presto.
a 2.
div.
Quasi Presto.

a 2.
a 2.
sf
tr

M
M

Moderato pomposo.
(Die Viertel wie früher die Halben.)
(Le semiminime come prima le semimassime.)
a 2.
Muta in E.
a 2.
Moderato pomposo.
(Die Viertel wie früher die Halben.)
(Le semiminime come prima le semimassime.)

a 2.
in E.

a 2.
tr

a 2.
a 2.
tr
tr
tr

Stretto. Molto animato.
a 2.
tr
fp
Stretto. Molto animato.

a 2.
a 2.
tr
fp
tr
fp

a 2.
a 2.

tr
tr

FRANZ LISZTS
SYMPHONISCHE DICHTUNGEN 1 u. 2

REVISIONSBERICHT

Im Jahre 1908 wurden in einer gemeinschaftlichen Sitzung der Revisoren, der Herausgeber und der Verleger die Leitgedanken und Grundsätze für eine vollständige, einheitliche und korrekte Gesamtausgabe der Werke Franz Liszts beraten und endgültig festgesetzt.

Aus praktischen Gründen der modernen Musikpflege mußten die vielfachen Unterschiede in der Benennung und Anordnung der Instrumente, in den Schlüsseln usw., vor allem aber sehr viele, für heutige Begriffe überflüssige oder selbst störende Versetzungszeichen beseitigt werden. Die auf letztere bezügliche Bestimmung lautet in endgültiger Fassung:

»Die von Liszt sehr reichlich angewendeten zufälligen Versetzungszeichen (namentlich Auflösungszeichen) sind für die heutige Praxis zum Teil entbehrlich geworden. Die nicht unbedingt notwendigen sind nur da beizubehalten, wo sie das Lesen tatsächlich noch erleichtern, Mißverständnisse verhüten oder für das harmonische Bild Lisztscher Schreibweise besonders charakteristisch erscheinen.«

Um jede Willkür auszuschliessen, sind alle irgendwie nennenswerten Änderungen, Weglassungen, Zusätze im Wortlaut der Lisztschen Partitur im Revisionsbericht je bei der betreffenden Komposition besonders aufgeführt und begründet worden, sodaß jeder mit der alten und der neuen Ausgabe in der Hand sich sein Urteil selbst bilden kann. Alle Zutaten, insbesondere Vortragsbezeichnungen, wurden in Klammern ( ) oder [ ] gesetzt; in einzelnen Fällen kann und soll dies nachträglich noch geschehen.

Die Herausgabe der Symphonischen Dichtungen war ursprünglich von Herrn Eugen d'Albert übernommen worden, der jedoch wegen anderweitiger großer Inanspruchnahme zurücktrat, nachdem er den Stich aller 12 Werke nur in erster Lesung hatte beaufsichtigen können. Die genaue Nachprüfung übernahm in dankenswerter Weise Herr Otto Taubmann in Berlin, in stetem Einvernehmen mit dem Kustos des Liszt-Museums, Herrn Hofrat Dr. Obrist, als dem Obmann der Revisionskommission.

BAND 1

CE QU'ON ENTEND SUR LA MONTAGNE.

Symphonische Dichtung Nr. 1*).

Vorlage: 1. Die erste Partiturausgabe, erschienen 1857 bei Breitkopf & Härtel in Leipzig. Verlagsnummer 9382.

2. Die autographe Partitur im Liszt-Museum in Weimar. Diese Originalhandschrift bot jedoch keine Grundlage für die Revision, da sie erheblich von der gestochenen Partitur abweicht. Liszt hat offenbar später vor dem Druck wesentliche Änderungen vorgenommen.

Bemerkungen:

S. 8. In der gedruckten Vorlage fehlen bei den Hörnern vom 4. zum 5. Takt die Bögen, die sich an derselben Stelle bei Hoboen und Fagotten finden. Als vermutlich versehentlich fortgelassen wurden diese Bögen hinzugefügt.

S. 10. Das *Crescendo* der gr. Trommel führt in der gedruckten Vorlage nicht zu einem dynamischen Höhepunkt. Als solcher wurde die ganze Note im 3. Takt angenommen und der erreichte Stärkegrad durch ein hinzugefügtes *mf* näher bezeichnet.

S. 39. Das 3. Horn hat in der gedruckten Vorlage im 2. Takt und im 8. Takt die Vorschrift »gestopft«. Da anzunehmen ist, daß die ganze Stelle gestopft zu blasen ist, wurde die zweite Vorschrift als irreführend gestrichen.

S. 41 Die gedruckte Vorlage hat für die 3. Posaune im 3. bis 6. Takt nach dem Buchstaben I die von allen anderen Instrumenten abweichende Vortragsbezeichnung:

Das wurde in Übereinstimmung mit der sonstigen Bezeichnung dieser Stelle geändert in:

S. 91. In der gedruckten Vorlage findet sich hier die Anmerkung: »Die Hörner-, Trompeten- und Posaunen-Fanfaren mäßig, aber nicht roh.« Da das Wort »mäßig« keinen verständlichen Sinn ergibt, wurde angenommen, daß es »massig« (engl. »prominent«, frz. »très-sonore«) heiße und ein Druckfehler vorliege.

* * *

*) Die in diesem Berichte zu den Symphonischen Dichtungen Nr. 1. bis 4 (erster und zweiter Band der Gesamtausgabe der Symphonischen Dichtungen) gemachten Bemerkungen haben auf die vorliegende Gestalt der genannten Werke keinen Bezug, da beide Bände bereits veröffentlicht waren, als eine Nachprüfung ihres Inhalts im Sinne der für die Gesamtausgabe maßgebenden Leitsätze zu jenen Bemerkungen Anlaß gab. Die betreffenden Änderungen können erst bei einem etwaigen Neudruck in die Platten eingetragen werden.
Otto Taubmann.

TASSO, LAMENTO E TRIONFO.

Symphonische Dichtung Nr. 2.

Vorlage: Die erste Partiturausgabe, erschienen 1856 bei Breitkopf & Härtel in Leipzig. Verlagsnummer 9136.

Bemerkungen:

S. 1. Auf Seite 177 der 1885 erschienenen Bandausgabe (Symphonische Dichtungen Nr. 1 bis 4, Volksausgabe Breitkopf & Härtel Nr. 517) findet sich folgende Bemerkung des Komponisten: Der Schluß-Satz kann ohne das Vorhergehende von Seite 223 Buchstabe H *Allegro con molto brio*, separat aufgeführt werden.

S. 1. Es dürfte interessieren, daß Liszt hier ganz ausnahmsweise ausdrücklich 2 Ventiltrompeten vorgeschrieben hat.

S. 4. In der gedruckten Vorlage fehlt für Einsatz der Streicher und der Hoboe im letzten Takt die Angabe des Stärkegrades. Im Hinblick auf die Angabe »*mf*« der Vorlage für Flöte und Klarinette im 4. Takt auf S. 5 erhielten auch die oben genannten Instrumente ein »*mf*«.

S. 6. Der Deutlichkeit wegen erhielten die Rhythmen ♩ ♪ der Violinen und Bratschen im 1. bis 4. Takt die in der Vorlage nicht enthaltene Form ♩ ♪.

S. 9. In der gedruckten Vorlage steht bei den Streichern vom 3. Takte an die Vorschrift »*cresc. e sempre più agitato e stringendo*«; bei den Bläsern fehlt diese Vorschrift. Da sie sich auf den Vortrag der ganzen Stelle bezieht, wurde sie über und unter das Gesamtsystem der Partitur gesetzt, bei den Streichern jedoch entfernt. Die Vorschrift »*ed agitato*« bei den Bläsern auf S. 10, 2. Takt wurde dadurch überflüssig gemacht und gleichfalls weggelassen.

S. 12 hat die gedruckte Vorlage im 6. Takt bei der Klarinette ein »*rit.*«, das durch die gleichzeitige Angabe *ritard.* über und unter dem Gesamtsystem der Partitur als überflüssig erschien und deshalb gestrichen wurde.

S. 17. Die gedruckte Vorlage hat im letzten Takt bei Violoncell I die Bezeichnung »Solo«. Da es sich hier augenscheinlich nicht um die Wiedergabe der Stelle durch ein Violoncello, sondern vielmehr um den solistischen Vortrag der Kantilene durch alle ersten Violoncelle handelt, wurde die irreführende Bezeichnung gestrichen.

S. 55, 5. Takt ff. Hier lag der bei S. 9 erwähnte Fall vor, der in gleicher Weise behandelt wurde.

S. 59. In der gedruckten Vorlage ist die Taktart für das *Allegro con molto brio* (Buchstabe H) mit C angegeben. Dagegen hat Liszts erstes Manuskript ₵. Demgemäß ist die Angabe der Vorlage in ₵ geändert worden.

* * *

www.ingramcontent.com/pod-product-compliance
Lightning Source LLC
LaVergne TN
LVHW061336060426
835511LV00014B/1948

* 9 7 8 1 6 0 8 7 4 0 2 2 2 *